Small Talk

Gordon Carrega

For Ulla

Small Talk
© 2016 by Gordon Carrega (carrega@gmx.de)
Photos by Ursula Schorn. Design by Petra Reisdorf
Published by Books on Demand GmbH, Norderstedt
Printed in Germany
ISBN: 9783743140295

CONTENTS

9	Night Owls
10	Didn't Spend
11	Stones
12	Empty Day
13	Your Voice
14	Enjoy
15	Just Talent
16	What
17	Never Think
18	Flowers
19	Forever
20	Here Comes
21	On My Way
22	Calm
23	The Same
24	Mutual
25	Hope
26	I Will
27	One Glove
28	But Actually
29	In My Arms
30	Exactly
31	Beginnings
32	No More
33	So What
34	I'll Be There
35	That's That

I would like to thank the Berlin-based video artist Wenfeng Liao. His work was the inspiration for two lines in the poem **In My Arms**. The lines are:
"Even my spurs can't make my desk chair gallop."
"One flower in the wind like a metronome gone mad."

Gordon Carrega lives in Berlin, Germany. He has published five previous books: **Back Gate, A Place to Stay, Life of the Party, Up Ahead,** and **Excursions.**

In all the world
There is no way whatever.
The stag cries even
In the most remote mountains.

Fujiwara No Toshinari
translated by Kenneth Rexroth

NIGHT OWLS

Night owls on the prowl mix their metaphors and don't give a hoot. I'm Ok for now, that's enough for now. Birthday parties keep happening, usually after sundown. Choose your reality, face up to it.

I went out of my way in order to get out of the way. Disorganizing my organized thoughts, I'm now aware of what I wasn't aware of previously. A postcard from no one has finally arrived. Do you love me now that I can dance?

Seeing as how I already see and wait, I'll now wait and see. Don't bother me with before and after, later is just fine. Nietzsche wrote that his whole philosophy was about rising above resentment.

Nostalgia, using the past wisely. The world's a stage, you're on next. Nothing to worry about, worry about the nothing. Let me hear your voice. All men are brothers, that's the problem. At the moment I'm not thinking of anyone.

Thanks for cleaning my reading glasses. I can now see the spaces between the lines. Too tired today to be impulsive. The soup is on. I mean, soup's on. The performance left me to my own resources, my empty mind, though casting my glance variously at the folks in the audience I was also performing right there in my seat.

If I were to trust what I feel I would be crazy by now. During the day do what you can to take care of your health, at night do what you can to ruin your health. I had meant what I said, however saying I was sorry eased my conscience.

Onward, ever onward. Go ahead while I stagger along, staying right here. Nod wisely, squint a bit, even if you don't get what I'm saying. Asked the neighbours speaking loudly outside my bedroom window if they would mind shutting up, seemed they did mind.

When will the spirit move me? Walking alone in the wide field I scatter my words, crows circling overhead, cawing in harmony. I didn't have to turn out to be the way I am but that's who I am.

Today I need a certain arrogance not to lose my mind. Time is not the same for all of us even when it's the same time.

DIDN'T SPEND

Didn't spend the day, the day never occurred to me. Because onto yourself. Correction, be a cause onto yourself. Neither of us knew what to say, we agreed on not knowing. An invitation from a friend to see a particular film, the film being important to him, should I go as an act of friendship even though the film doesn't interest me?

Leaving for holiday, looking forward to my return. The novel was hard to follow as I read the pages in sequence, switched to reading every other page. Strolling home, summer twilight, just me on the sidewalk of the street where I live, the usual bus slowly passing, well-lit inside and no passengers, I feel weightless, floating in the glow of the old familiar.

What's preferable, knowing nothing or not knowing anything? Stayed in all day yesterday, bored and restless, wishing for somewhere to go. Today a few appointments, already miss my yesterday. He informed me that I only knew half the story, didn't say which half nor did he tell me the other half.

Standing to put on my black Levis, fell to the floor, entangled in the pants' legs. Told I looked sad, answered I didn't feel sad. Assured that I certainly looked sad, looked in the mirror, I did look rather sad, decided to go ahead and feel sad.

Trust is mystical. She turned away from me then smiled or did she smile then turn away, happened so fast. A glass of wine in the café, reading the menu over and over again from cover to cover for I had forgotten my book.

No advice, simply tell me what to do. Music called the blues helps you to overcome the blues while you tear your hair out, that's the idea. Did you see what I just saw? Rise above or rise below.

Discussing the opinions of someone who is already dead, can I say I agree with him, or must I use the past tense, saying, for example, I always agreed with him, or I used to agree with him? Can I still agree with someone who's already dead?

STONES

I told him how exhilarating it had been to watch the video of the Rolling Stones performing in Cuba, he replied that he didn't like the Rolling Stones. Targeted by the wish of no story. Let's wait until the bus comes.

Looked back, so did he, we didn't wave. Duration of arrival, possessed by I am here. List of things to do, etc. etc. etc. Dark blue, right colour for never. Back in town for a few days, phoned an old friend from the hotel lobby.

Youth being overrated, doing my best to be the old man that I am. Practice your charm, be charming. Went out, returned a few minutes later to write down a fragment of thought, forgot what it was, stared at the blank white page as if my memory lurked hidden in the whiteness.

Asked my body if I'd ever been original, felt no pain. To visit or to make a visit? Fire doesn't wait. Don't make me laugh! He said I shouldn't make him laugh. She'd appreciate if I brought flowers, didn't say what kind of flowers.

Going to not. Not what? Simply not. Never lend money to friends unless they ask. Turned my head to glance into the mirror, no mirror in that place on the wall where I'd expected a mirror, my footsteps tripped on the worn-out carpet.

A café where only couples are allowed, each couple at a separate table, talking to each other not permitted, eating, drinking in their own silence until all the different silences of all the different couples intermix and belong to no particular couple.

No good for myself. A year has gone by, a year for all concerned. Language is whatever we say, contradictions and all. I leave early, rushing isn't for me. Change the way we think, change the way we feel.

Looking for a road to ruin with stopping-off points for a bit of sightseeing. I still go to that place in my thoughts that she used to inhabit, now learning to communicate with the no one there. I should go back but I can't.

Remarks too close to home, not so close to home, depends on my mood. Whose voice that is I think I know, could be wrong. Not doing myself any good.

EMPTY DAY

Another empty day, no news that someone I know has died. Always prepared to talk about myself, what else but me-ness? I keep hearing a clicking sound, something's clicking in my apartment. I've looked around, refuse to keep looking, go ahead, keep clicking.

Fooled them all, they thought I was one of them. Today such beauty all around me, same old same perfect as it is, even my mistakes have a transcendent glow. My best friend and I constantly insult each other.

Don't know what to do next, can always do it later. Jesus had only one cross to bear. Said to myself, I'm just so tired. Are you really? asked a voice from nowhere. Black T-shirt when I go out, grey T-shirt at home.

Missing the glass when pouring my wine, blindness in one eye. I like her enthusiasm, she doesn't like mine, dashed hopes. See you this evening when the wind picks up. Losing my mind which in the first place never belonged to me anyway.

Alone, staring at the full moon, my loneliness like a radiant moon garment. Self-confident, enthusiastic, who needs depth of character? I practice looking tired. What happens, what doesn't happen, one life, don't take it personally, though it is said you should stand up for yourself when insulted.

Washed the clothes, hung them out, now they're dry. I need what I'm getting, not getting what I need. Is love personal or transcendental? Darkness, darkness, can't find the light switch. The very comfort of you and me being alike says it all.

Takes a bit of time to experience the thrill of being alone. Fragments of thought. I always know where my keys are. A wine taster or a wine drinker?

Ran into Walt Whitman, "Hey Walt, how you doing?" "If I contradict myself, I contradict myself," he said. "You've said that already," I said. "Nothing new," he answered.

YOUR VOICE

Keep talking, your voice adds a certain something though all has already been said. Who I am, a feeling of who I am, confidential relationship with myself. Not all stories have an end. I love my life, freedom to wash my hands.

Dear friends, when I'm dying gather round me, take turns singing stay just a little bit longer, please, please, please tell me that you're gonna. Oh won't you stay just a little bit longer. Not believing what I don't believe, note my determined posture.

A wax museum of doubt and despair. On my lunch hour, seeing a prostitute on the corner I'm overwhelmed with thoughts of Mary Magdalene, my out to lunch epiphany. Losing interest in sitting with friends in a café, what's left, a walk in nature, a monastery?

First understand, then blame. She's so delightful, I feel helpless. Inclined to mysticism, sunglasses at night to analyse auras. Speaking of suicide, don't do it unless you want to.

What I say isn't necessarily true. Excuse the disturbance, I'm a disturbed person. Took a walk in the rain to wonder is there a problem. Practice generic thinking.

Infatuation doesn't get the credit it deserves. No, I never hear right. Tired of missing you, now I lay me down to weep. Which one of my black T-shirts should I wear today? I'm not late yet but I will be.

The pleasure of no one to come home to. Not everybody sees things from my perspective. No solution, try an alternative. The reason is no reason. Let's hark back to the moment that has just passed. Agreeing, disagreeing same stream of consciousness.

A person being more than what's evident, I'm free of accomplishments, yet everything's Ok for now while going on until it ends. Don't need any more interesting people in my life, a limit to pleasure, though so many fascinating individuals, enough is really enough, and no one around to ask why or why not.

ENJOY

I enjoy my life, I don't enjoy my life, what a life. Stand up straight, look me in the eye, do your best, hope your best is good enough. My body isn't really me. At the party we discussed the names of rivers in Africa.

Walking home at twilight, deserted tree-covered sidewalk, the day like a cloud behind me, I pass my house, keep going, the end of the sidewalk nowhere in sight, darkness does fall.

Drinking a glass of wine at the cafe, shall I sit upright, legs crossed, or shall I be leaning on the table, hunched over, huddled in myself, or shall I sit back in the chair, legs outstretched, or shall my legs be decently together, feet on the floor, sunglasses, of course sunglasses.

Love me, don't fall in love with me. Arguing about memories. Although no one we knew had died, we held a wake, an empty coffin surrounded by mourners, a practice run for us mourners. I have my reasons, somewhere in my mind, regret always for later.

Waiting, pure waiting. We don't have to go over that all over again, that's for sure. Mirror, mirror on the wall doesn't give a damn. I am at home, you at your home, I'm saddened by the word home.

The human condition, outdated. This moment, not a difficult moment. I'm not busy, busy mind. Go where you belong. Hi, it's me, how you doing, what are you struggling with?

Always so full of surprises, must take practice. Nonetheless, let's praise the word nonetheless. Laugh or don't laugh, same difference. A bottle of wine, a glint in my eye. Finally fit and ready to go, one of these days.

I understand you, it's myself I don't understand. Screaming children in the playground, scream children, scream. I asked the dish-washer if he'd had a hard day at the office.

A true story doesn't always actually happen. If my behaviour is obvious to you and not obvious to me, be subtle. Our first night together, she brought her dog.

JUST TALENT

Just talent nothing but talent. We promised to forget each other. I spent my teenage years hanging out on the corner. Now I'm obliged to finish the bottle of wine.

I have already taken off my sunglasses. Because everybody's having a good time doesn't mean I have to. Hush now, don't exclaim. Later the very same day and I don't save for later.

Used to listen to music, now I just listen. I like you, don't like being with you. Let's wait and see. As the world turns, turn of phrase.

Don't know what it is, take it on trust. It sure is something so live with the word it, Maybe it matters, maybe it doesn't, maybe I don't even mean it. Those dear old friends we neither see nor long for.

Writers and their work. I used to work in a factory. Suffering along, going my way, getting sentimental over you whoever you are. Insist on being modest. My inner voice hasn't aged much. A true story that never happened.

The couple on line in front of me are discussing their holiday plans. Your hand cold or not cold, your hand. Decided to be inconsistent, no one decides to be incontinent. Déjà vu, I'll get there on my own.

Is the memory of never meeting you a new memory? A free day, free to be puzzled about what to do. Would you mind dimming that blinding light at the end of the tunnel?

Just wait, forget about waiting for. Don't even learn to wait, just wait. You told me so, so what? Come sit here beside me. Didn't think of that. If I'd thought of that I'd be there now.

I was brought up, could have been a bit further up. His name, what's his name, learned he didn't have one. Talking to myself, saying now we'll get up and go, meaning now I will get up and go, knowing that now will soon be relegated to when or if.

WHAT

The deaf old man shouts what, what and the dogs bark their orders all afternoon. Full moon, crescent moon, whatever moon, same old moon lasting a lifetime. They also serve who only stand and wait so I get what I deserve. Always let me know where you are.

The Dadaists didn't really mean it. I like to be where I'm going. All I know about him is his loud laugh. I don't need to tell the difference between this and that. Make sense for sense does not exist unless you make it.

Blame me, let me stand at the crossroads of blame and more blame. Can a question be asked without a question mark in the voice? Every night he reads himself to sleep and he hopes one night to read himself to death.

Holding hands still in fashion. No words can describe how I spent the day. I'm just bragging. Come on over, bring your guitar. A lecture on modesty and revolution, how to be a modest revolutionary.

I sit in the lakeside café, a cigarillo, a glass of wine, soon she will return from her swim, ask for a sip of my wine, ask for some smoke blown in her direction, for she so enjoys the smoke from my cigarillo. The difference between knowing and not knowing, the unknown always nearby, an empty chair.

A passing fancy that forgot to pass. Just one mood after another. Meaning of random as in a random moment. Home is where my drunken stagger took me, I staggered home.

Someone at the door, joie de vivre. I admire her independence, she admires my dependence. Don't knock over the one glass of wine you allow yourself in the evening.

Forgot to laugh. Insights rather than judgements. I had a good time and didn't enjoy myself. Don't blame me for falling in love with you. Nobody's perfect, we have friends.

Went back to be sure there was nothing burning, went back to be sure, went back again just to be sure. Nothing's always burning.

NEVER THINK

Without you I would never think of taking a walk in the rain. I wear a jacket even in hot weather to keep checking my pockets. Relationship means worship in the temple of togetherness.

Voices speaking of all that was, sunlight in the window of an old house. These days I don't hear much about loneliness, must be outdated. I won't give him the pleasure of my not saying hello, and if I never saw him again it would be too soon.

Wanting doesn't have to be knowing what I want. I'm not drunk now, drunk a few minutes ago. Where am I, where is it, where are you, where are we going, and how about somewhere, anywhere, where ever, nowhere? Sadness taking hold for the very word nowhere.

Sunny afternoon, walking briskly along the sidewalk, an old man comes toward me, tottering along with his cane, offers a diffident smile, his cloudy eyes peer shyly at me, slight wave of his hand like a question, does he dare to be here? I nod and keep going, eternity at my back.

My best friend is the nicest guy I know, the damn phoney. I don't remember chopping down the cherry tree. What I mean to say might be different to what my words mean. A choice of nightmares, I'll decide later.

And what if there was no last time? I've already crossed the bridge, now I have to come to it. Give me Jesus without the story. We had different ideas about what it meant to stroll around the city.

He talked constantly about his boundaries and finally that's what he became, a boundary. The waitress forgot my saucer. Went home, sat on my balcony, listening to the barking dogs. I think so therefore I am. Nothing happens behind my back.

I used to have a plan, needed more than a plan. Your opinion is not one of the details regarding what actually happened. A life free of meaning, I always have time for melancholy.

She asked me if I still remembered the cry of the peacocks. I asked what peacocks? She said she had mixed me up with the other guy. Now I keep hoping to hear the cry of the damn peacocks.

FLOWERS

Flowers grow even in places where no one ever goes. I'm not screaming, its only a magnificent yawn. What I like about you is what I like about you, don't ask why. I put on my shoes, my shoes know where to take me..

I have my own life I mutter to myself and a profound silence comes over me as if fallen from the heavens, stopping me in my tracks. The waitress sauntering to my table brought my hunger for her.

Ambivalence as good a way as any. I'm also a certain type. Got the news that tomorrow is another day, I'm on the look-out. All is love but my brain needs a bit more time. When I talk with my ninety-year-old neighbour, he talks only about himself.

Again switching on the light that doesn't work, victim of habit. Move over Beethoven. I told you not to trip on the worn-out carpet. Seeking my share of quiet desperation I go out among the masses.

Examine your imagination in order to sort out the figments from what's real imagination. Going all the way back to make sure my door is locked I just love my locked door. Take my hand take my whole life too.

Somewhere the best line for me to stand on. Almost could be good enough, then comes not always. A long time since I last sat on the well-worn wooden floor, now my father's chair is unoccupied. Different people do awaken different feelings in us.

Transcendence is an experience not a belief. Surprise mistaken for disapproval. I've forgotten why I don't like him. Used to call my mother every New Year's Eve at midnight on the dot. Wanting what I want, wanting what you want, same wanting.

I still recall that spring evening I first walked the street of loneliness. The difference between having a friend and having a friendship. This building I now live in won't be standing when I return from the dead.

FOREVER

The word forever, the limits of language in telling you I will love you forever so I say always. Unless you're OK being continually amazed, his amazing intellect will wear you down. At least you're puzzled, I didn't get that far.

When you wash your hands be sure to wash between your fingers you sneaky devil. How long is long enough for two old friends to keep looking deeply into each other's eyes as they converse?

Not difficult to make a list of what not to do when you're broke. Please don't feel like a victim of my kindness. First thing in the morning she watered the flowers on her balcony. On my balcony no flowers, just memories.

I told him I love my life, he heard lost. I can do one thing not one thing after another. Busy avoiding what doesn't exist. Just look at the paintings, don't ask the artist any questions. Again today, it's today again, once again this particular today, down the stairs and up the stairs.

Write to remember write to forget. What's the opposite of memoir? She still refers to our first night in the hotel room when right after our lovemaking I got out of bed to wash out my white shirt for the next day's meeting.

I thought I was interrupting you, didn't know our conversation was already over. On the sightseeing tour I loitered behind, enjoying the cool breeze. You can envy anybody if you try hard enough. Born with the fear of death. Are you lonely, very lonely?

Getting lost is part of knowing where I'm going. Another passer-by and then another and another, when will it end? The ghost that trails behind me reminding me of problems I don't have.

We had met often enough for him to forget my name. To love a drunk you must be kind, saintly, and heroic. Now he will praise who you are, do not disappoint yourself.

That first time the Neanderthal experienced a bewildering sense of beauty as he stared up at the full-moon, he sat on his boulder, called for his woman to sit close to him, placed his arms around her, grunted in an unusual way to let her know a new intimacy was occurring.

HERE COMES

Here comes another bon vivant. I can rely on my voice asking or not asking tennis anyone? A white shirt all alone on the clothesline. Practicing the loud cackling laughter of someone who has nothing to lose.

Confused, desperate, I asked the Lord to help me find my way. The Lord replied, you have already found your way. Another sleepless night. On the table in the hot sun a burning candle, for this too shall pass, the past having the character of a former now.

Another photograph of myself grinning as I open the door. I used to read a lot and now I just read. The cacophony of birds chirping and singing disturbs my peace of mind. What's the reason for all this? All this, the reason is all this.

I stop to look around, same old same. You carry whatever you carry, certainly you carry yourself. The disordered papers on my desk, I chuckle when I can't find what I know for sure is there.

The author is old now, and his body no longer works so well, though he's very proud of his body of work. Waking up late on Sunday morning, the usual hangover, the usual phone calls to apologize for my drunken behaviour at the party.

Smiling when I collide with another passenger on the bus, singing to myself got a smile on my face for the whole human race. I'm not dead yet, finally knowing who I am, being as usual too distracted to examine my life.

Put your faith in the story and then forget about both faith and story, getting carried away by what you're saying. Concentration is overrated, though I'm still a miner working in the language mine.

Faithful to a forgotten promise, just keep going. I embraced her. She said don't. I said you don't want it, then give it back, give me back my embrace. Call me the nowhere man behind my back.

I seem to be running late. Seem, what do you mean by seem? The human body knows no bounds. Didn't you hear me say I am sorry, how many times must I say I am sorry?

ON MY WAY

I hold my breath while I tie my shoes. On my way to the party, am I already a guest or am I a guest when I arrive? Get dressed, forget your problems. She's using me but not using me enough.

Being right is no excuse for not being compassionate and I'm not arrogant enough to ask who I am without this constant inner voice. My lack of understanding, much more convincing than your lack of understanding.

We have a deep personal friendship but don't take it personally. Tired of everything, I'm now amused rather than concerned. Looks good, tastes good, smells good, feels good, sounds good, my own life now lives me since I've come to my senses.

If you have no food at home and you go out to eat and meet the woman you end up marrying your meeting was happenstance and your being hungry and having no food at home were the circumstances that allowed the happenstance to occur. Now deal with the results.

Sunny weather so we go for a walk in nature. Yesterday, a cloudy day, we went for a walk in the same nature. Where did you put the oranges? My daily routine suddenly so unfamiliar that I feel ecstatic not knowing where to go.

In the job announcement for an executioner no previous experience necessary. Who cares what's meant by freedom, I know when to panic and when not to. The philosopher has secretly changed his mind.

Still hoping to see the error of my ways, doubt and uncertainty always welcome. If it weren't for you I would lie down right now and die. I focus on neither what is nor what isn't. Is there something I should know? Know thyself.

Please tell me where the time goes. Time, I need time. Oh my God I am sorry and beg pardon for all my sins, homage to my catholic childhood. Come, come, come said the old woman to her husband who could barely walk.

Ceaseless repetition of gestures initiated by others, what goes around comes around, the eternal return. Socrates said that he felt pity for any man who had never crawled after a woman. The wide blue sky, all my own.

CALM

So very calm as if someone had blown out my pilot light, I asked her if I could become a picture on her bedroom wall. The homeless guy walks up to me out of the blue and says I shouldn't worry because I'm exactly who I'm supposed to be, then he moved on to someone else.

Better to be blamed for something I did or something I didn't do? I need what I'm getting, not getting what I need. Tired of everything, I myself am not tired. I explain, I don't solve. Laughter is laughter even if you pretend.

On a bright sunny day, waiting at the window with eyes closed, I decide to shoot myself because I can't find my sunglasses. I'm not complicated, it's my thinking. I was disappointed when she didn't show up for our appointment.

Words, I have words, and of course language as well as a one-of-a-kind attitude. I don't have the courage to quit but if I got fired I would have the strength to deal with it.

Possessed by desire, I lie down and indulge my fantasies while she makes her soup in which my waiting is the main ingredient. Instead, instead, one instead after another.

The saxophone player on the subway played a deep rendition of You've Got A Friend, making me a bit tearful, the woman across the aisle offering a slight commiserating smile before discretely glancing away.

Basking neither in the sun nor in glory. At first I wasn't sure that I would love you forever. Two o'clock in the morning, feeling ecstatic, who can I call. Facts, who cares about facts. Can you please help me to relieve the rigmarole of knowing myself.

Making friends is pretty much the same for everybody though people are different and you need friends. I'm always holding on, prepared to fall. The outdoors, how empty it seems, trees and so on.

I know I'm crazy, trust my knowing. Get dressed, OK, I'll get dressed. The whole story is we took a walk together one rainy afternoon. He's dead now, the old friend who used to say to thine own self be true.

THE SAME

Having shared the same experiences that we don't remember, now begins the whatever. I'm always somewhere, at times I'm here when you need me, though I might not pass this way again and I'm not so interested in if as in if you need me.

I told the street musician that I liked his playing but didn't have any change in my pocket. A dream in which I'm too old to die. Praise the Lord, praise the Lord. Fine, said the Lord, but that does not create in me a sense of obligation.

He likes to speak but communicating isn't all that important. I was the first to walk through the forest after the rain. She reminded me of someone I needed to know and she remembered me from the ship that had sailed without me. I don't understand walking fast. Waiting isn't everything but it sure is something. Saying sorry too often is quite Ok.

Even the busy signal on her phone fills me with delight. Go home and slam all the doors. One thing after another until there's nothing left. I said he could trust me and I knew that was all I had to offer him.

Now we will dismantle the truth which is merely a convenient version. I have two good friends, one is antagonistic and the other too nice. Try to avoid saying of course and at all costs avoid saying of course not.

Is there still something to learn or am I really who I appear to be? A new kind of wine called Nirvana. Washing my hands and again washing my hands in the same stream. I feel driven when I ride my bicycle.

At his funeral I forgot what he had done for a living. Same old conversation or same old silence. Is this it or is that it, it being a baffling two letter word, not to mention this or that.

He's crazy, knows he's crazy, and they want to have him committed although he himself is not committed to being crazy. You have no proof that I said what I said. Sadness, let's celebrate our sadness.

MUTUAL

On our last night together we compared our mutual indifference. Fall back on your mistakes. Polishing my shoes I remember the weak arms of my father. Several months now into their relationship, she calls him Monsieur and the rest of us stare in unison in his direction.

The cost of living, shoelaces, for example. I devote myself to the full-time occupation of explaining myself to myself. When she modeled her new outfit, a tight, short, low-cut red dress purchased for her holiday in Italy, we couldn't help but inquire if she planned to spend the summer in Rome working as a streetwalker.

Everyone looks familiar, one day turns into the next. A constant look to see what's happening. A minimalist in art as well as in lovemaking. Her eyes, her wide, delicate eyes, the subtle inflections of her eyes as she expresses doubt, for example.

Let's ruin our health, good health isn't everything. We don't get along, except for walking the dog together in the evening and we don't even have a dog. She refused me permission to look at other women when we were out together.

I don't have any special interests, any special way to spend my free time, but I often stop suddenly and spin around a few times when walking in the street. My mind stands in the way of further possibilities.

I don't want to end up being just who I am. I am addicted so when I do what I do I have to do it. The homeless old man asked for some words of wisdom, just a few words of wisdom.

I know I seem lost in oblivion, I'm just dealing with disappointment. This afternoon at the outdoor café, smiling at my last glass of wine. Welcome to the brotherhood of aloneness.

The truth, being direct with the truth, that's not my mission. Powerless, finally powerless, what a relief. Asked to explain myself I could only answer I had never said that I knew myself, take it from there.

If I die on a morning like this one the birds will continue singing. Let's take turns.

HOPE

Hoping to find myself dead when I wake up in the morning, I drift off into another night of sound sleep. That's that, he said. Ok, we replied, gawking at our new source of wisdom.

Looking all over the place for the glasses I'm already wearing. Some days living in fear, some days living with fear. Bodily pleasure, pretty much the same, yet so much depends on who I'm giving it to and getting it from.

That afternoon, wandering together around the city, observing and remembering, entranced, revisiting our familiar places, it's like we're visiting from the hereafter, I said. We're all ghosts already so we should wise up and live with that knowledge, she said.

I'd like to be the eternal guest sleeping on the couch. They say life is fleeting so it must have left without me, though I still have my clock. Fooling everybody is a lot better than fooling no one. No more wild nights, what a relief.

Settled into the new life and it's all so terribly familiar. Please hand me the microphone. I said give me the damn microphone. I insist on my freedom to lock myself in. Is this now or is it then?

What a relief to hear you've never loved me. I was afraid you had lost your mind when you dashed wildly out the door. Praise the Lord for the word finale. I meant to read your new book, had a cup of tea instead, spent the afternoon in reverie.

Nothing anybody can do about it. Not anybody? Nobody. Not even a somebody? Let's go. Go where? Wherever. I'm practicing being laconic. Excuse me, I said to the attractive woman, I didn't mean to brush against you. Is that what you did, brush against me?

Vivacious, a good word to describe her and when something gets said that's not in accord with her bright outlook, her face goes blank. I broke into a wild sprint to catch the bus, passing the old man limping along, hoping to catch the very same bus.

Haunted by the ghost of myself, must everything have a name?

I WILL

I will die, future, I died, past, I'm dead, present. Vanity's got me practicing my dead look in front of the mirror. I made a decision and don't ask if I'm sure it's the right one. Don't turn on the light when you find me sitting in a dark room next to an unlit candle. I always have matches in my pocket.

I need neither meaning nor purpose, barely get through the day. Logic or impulse, choose one. A door closes and then another in the same house. No yesterday in your journal, leave a few blank pages, dated or undated.

I am guilty so I don't have to feel guilty. Looking forward to not talking to anybody at the party. Actually I'm quite fine. Actually, why actually? Because I live in the actual. If you don't know what to do next you've come to the right place. Go ahead, take your time, we'll wait.

The nothing that is and the nothing that isn't, I can still tell the difference. I haven't received her love letter, she must still be working on it. Nowhere to go and plenty of time to get there.

What a life, did I fall into it? Wasn't the fall, was the sudden stop. What a pleasure it is to wonder why. Talking to someone whose suffering is exactly like mine. As the Buddhists say, life is suffering and then you die.

Don't treat me like a fool, I said. I thought you liked when I treated you like a fool, she answered. Only sometimes, I replied. I am dying to find out just what it is that I don't know. How did you manage to get here before I did, did you know the way?

It's fun talking to you, let's keep it going or have we already said what needs to be said. What happens, happens, so forget about next as in what happens next. I promise that today I will look outward rather than inward.

Passion, he said, that's my driving force, a life of passion. I replied that I have no driving force, I simply await joy. Here in our modern city a castle is being rebuilt to give us back our history.

I told her that I couldn't imagine being in a relationship with anyone other than her. She replied that she couldn't imagine being in a relationship with anyone at all.

ONE GLOVE

One glove for the right hand, the other for the left hand, it isn't all that complicated. I used to want to be a wanderer, now I just walk around the neighbourhood, smiling at strangers.

The best way to silence him, put on some classical music, then he shuts his mouth, closes his eyes, does his best to look deeply gone into cultural sophistication. Something's wrong, I don't need a drink this evening.

No one seems to care about the results of my research on indifference. My new project, Signs of Life. When does not knowing become a mystery rather than just not knowing? Already late, all of me straining to get there.

Those days when what I don't want is all that remains. Another sleepless night wondering how many pages make a book. He suffered a great loss. Must loss be always so personal and ever-present as the world turns?

I feel good today though I have the same problems that I worried about all day yesterday. Are you lonely, very lonely? She's so beautiful that when we walk down the street together I have the urge to start limping.

Then I said to the angel who dropped by the other day to tell me that I'd been forgiven, I said to be forgiven is one thing to be blessed is something else entirely. You'll have to live with that, the angel answered, disappearing in thin air.

In my pocket the exact change but for what? There are forces known and unknown, my face, for example, mine but not all mine. Running free and no wind, always wanted to be free in the wind. Doing my best to answer questions before being asked.

Laughing off my headache with a good friend. The floor is tilted, when my pen falls off the desk I should remember to look across the room. I got home just in time as the crow flies.

One day I will no longer be here and that day will go on into the future as the future becomes the past to explain my not being here, cemeteries offer proof.

Then I realized she needed me to make sense when we conversed.

BUT ACTUALLY

I feel tired but actually I'm not, though I'm not is lost in the eternity of feeling and not feeling. The blank pages of my daily calendar do make me suspicious. I stand up only to wonder why I had stood up.

Ignore me and I still exist in the knowledge of what you don't want. The end of another day pretending to be exactly who I am, placing my faith in the ongoing discourse with myself. Here I am, I announced, offering full disclosure.

Who, what, why, how, when, where, which one stops you in your tracks? It has come to pass therefore we have the past tense not to mention the letters neither written nor sent. You will always occupy a special place in my sexual fantasies.

Vague memories can be useful. Holding up well in the face of the many faces which all look alike when the right mood descends. Why refuse to compromise when the word offers promise?

Hello old friend, come on by and let us stand shoulder to shoulder under the full moon. Now that all has been said, we now have now what. Let's live with this conclusion. A timeless experience takes place in the same old time.

You tell me you have moved elsewhere, my boat against the current and no light at the end of the pier. Please gang up on me and assure me that everything is Ok, though I am intrigued to know that I look like death warmed over.

Too much emphasis placed on what is meant by what has been said. Surrender to the experience of hearing, ask questions, make comments that lead to revelation. Who needs yearning? I have what I need.

Surviving the birth process we go from one process to another until the dying process. This morning I bought the daily newspaper, in the afternoon I again bought the same newspaper at a different news stand. Again, that word again simply hangs there in the sunlight.

My infirmities give me character and I just need a moment to change my shirt. It's not that I don't care, simply not interested.

IN MY ARMS

Please die in my arms, right here on the dotted line. Don't confuse forgetful with forgettable. Be here now with a focus on afterwards. Intoxicated by the memory of old friends, I smile at strangers.

Learning to ask for help keeps me going. With your notebook or prayer book, you are on your way to right here. I'm not at all interesting, that's my charm. One moment, then another moment, the rest is up to me.

Waves, the sound of waves breaking on a distant shore. Distant, why distant? We're right here at the seaside. I prefer the sound of what isn't right here, hence the distant shore.

Captivated, I count the minutes. Time is form and content. After all these years, still looking around like I just got here. More than one voice, voices. I feel like a man who has lost his dog.

Did you have your eyes on me all along? We don't notice what we don't notice, therefore memories are always worth talking about. No end to not now and not yet.

Daylight blows out the candle. One flower in the wind like a metronome gone mad. A caravan crossing the desert crossed my mind. Memory exhaustion. My habits keep me in the dark.

Coming round the mountain haunts my memory as well as take it off, take it off, take it off. Even my spurs can't make my desk chair gallop. Forgetting is a part of what happens. Think it through but my days are numbered so pick one.

Beginning right now, all is lullaby. Steady as I go, steadiness keeps me going. I place my faith in honesty and understand that the real pain involved in deception lies in being caught. I follow your discourse with the hope of being freed from understanding.

Satisfied with what I already know, convinced that even more knowledge waits around the next corner, here I come. Are we now on the dance floor? What I'm dying to hear is up to you so use your judgement like on Judgement Day.

EXACTLY

You seem to be exactly who you are though of course this is only a practice run. Doesn't have to mean we know each other. Now, still another now, drowning in a sea of one now after another. In a case like this, add then, now and then, now and then, easy to dance to.

When he knew for sure that he was dying, he asked to be left in silence because he wanted to focus on the experience, to concentrate, he wanted to concentrate as death came along.

I don't remember your name but I remember everything else that happened, chalked up to experience but I can't find the notebook. What you have is what happens next.

Your role in all this fits well with the changes in the narrative as you continue to live within your means, comfortable with discomfort. I don't mean anything by that.

Beginning today at three pm I will feel elated for ten minutes. Tomorrow for twenty minutes. Next day for thirty minutes, until the end of time.

A sign directly above my head casts a shadow over me. Tilting my head back, straining my neck, just as I'm about to get a glance at the sign, it moves out of vision. Asking some passer-by what the sign says, most likely answer how should I know?

Freedom of mind, exactly which star are you looking at? Ashes fall, sometimes they remain in the air. Did you bring me or did I come with you? On the early bus to wherever.

Walk like a man, talk like a man. Thank you for your clear directions but I've changed my mind. Yes, it's real, my hand, my handwriting, your address, the distance.

Lying in wait, a story without a story line. I should change my life but my memory isn't all that good. Can I come over tonight? So long ago, must be dead by now.

Everybody likes somebody. Did you use to live on this street or are you once again influenced by the kindness of strangers?

BEGINNINGS

Incremental, an increase in number or amount while we talk about the beginning. Behind the scenes, a different scenario. Go ahead, saunter along, caught as you are in what you see or don't see. In foreground, the very next day got here before you. Who is that waving in the distance? Later I will examine the need for questions.

Let's not spend all our time looking for some kind of grief in asking whether this is the same as some other time. The preposition is for, wait for. You wanted to mention the right moment, distracted of course. Now the results, one word at a time, believing in what you believe. No one else the moment renewal happens.

The visitors to the museum, encounter with themselves. Gain or loss, the ongoing discourse. A stroll along the wayside of meaning. Feeling useless, how refreshing. These simple thoughts after all that time as ever before to kingdom come. Eyes looking forward has come to pass, including learning to know the somebody else in the very self.

What has already been spoken, gone astray. The very comfort of us being alike while we're kept waiting. Have I shown you my art work? Oh memory, you do exclaim. Let's remember the last time and conduct ourselves accordingly. Whether we say hello or not, it's a truism that sometimes we do and sometimes we don't.

Home is where, when you go there, they have to take you in. Don't take it personally. Come on, get going, tossed over my shoulder to the disappearing shadow. One idea or another leads to the word impromptu. When we meet has to be a place of some kind. The word encounter. Never has already happened.

I have to ask, I can't go on pretending to pretend. I called ahead to let them know, trusting my judgement at the last minute. Now the stillness, an occasion. Used to be a time when I did my share and shared my doing. A voice nearby insinuating bygones. An extended hunch within the eternal narrative. Stand aside said the doorman to the shadows.

A lot of moments to be discussed at a later date, one at a time. Who needs music to reveal what's up and coming? Episodes are contrived to allow me not to fall on my face. Now the hero on a fact-finding mission. Me and my decorated opinions even when I'm speechless one word at a time.

Answers lurking, needed or not. I'll always remember you taking notes and the image won't change to accommodate the next word or two. A word within a word, one word less. The following is followed and I keep being familiar. Plenty of time to warm up my cold shoulder before turning it in your direction.

NO MORE

If you don't know by now the difference between learning and unlearning, often confused with forgetting the same old something or the other, sometimes mixed up with yearning, and its opposite. Anyway, don't die yet.

Sitting alone in an otherwise empty row in a movie house, the feel of my hand in my empty mailbox, no one talking to me at the party, I realize I'm a divine entity here on earth to heal those folks who suffer from migraine.

Even sense is senseless so be careful not to trip while stepping aside or stepping outside. Yes, I do love repeating myself. Please, I beg you, for what I still don't know. I love repeating myself. Look me over once or twice. The nightmare of being consistent keeps me going.

When you arrive you seem already to be leaving. Is it the door, is the door the problem? I see what you're saying, no need to remove my sunglasses while keeping an eye on otherwise.

Stop and stare, don't notice what's there. A passing fancy in context.

Only with a full life can you know the meaninglessness of it all. Never is a shadow that falls over all that I do and I can't rely on temperament, for never is a shadow that's never witnessed. My strides, how they add up.

I am who I am regardless of facts against the wild sky. The truth is I thought I would be different, different somehow. This is the same as some other time in some other place. Some comfort, I exist.

The very word, answer! I break into tears, nothing to do with any question or smoke getting in my eyes, simply hearing the word, answer, a verb or a noun, the wonder of it all, my heart breaks, the tears flow.

Here comes the promise dressed up as once before, just in case in the ongoing seizure of myself I need to find out. I remember the bible class when I wanted to be the prodigal son returning home, must get an update, see how he's doing.

I don't have to take the most direct route, the future, being mainstream, one thing does lead to another, so don't blame me if I've forgotten your name. Explanations exist in the nerves and no one can correct me or tell me all has already been said.

SO WHAT

I have no destiny, so what! Did we converse or just exchange information? All is vicarious. Where am I, what am I supposed to be doing? The sign, waiting room.

No opinion, then no need to change your mind. You might think so but I don't know what to do about that because there's no what. We don't have everything and we have only one of everything we have.

With my neighbour for many years, a long conversation about his future plans, the one time we spoke on the day he moved out. The five senses in training all day long. We took our own sweet time, I took hers and she took mine.

One suicide carefully planned, the other on the spur of the moment. Do I prefer an excuse or a reason? We've never met, please believe me. Once again at the end of my rope, how many ropes do I have?

On my afternoon stroll, a lovely woman walks towards me, a complete stranger, this woman I've never been in love with, an empty space in my memory. Went to the cemetery, took a walk with easeful death.

The man sitting in the café this afternoon is not my old friend Jack and no one to talk with about this phenomenon. In concert with my wishes, we practiced being distracted, breaking the spell of what was really happening.

Walking around the corner, leaning on the birch tree, a sense of arrival. Another day, stalked by language. To be on time for my usual obscurity. Stepping aside, allowing everyone else to board the train before me. Why look out the train window at the fleeting landscape? Why put myself through this misery?

Of course I don't know why I do what I do, why should I, condemned as I am to being sure of myself. After great pain a formal feeling comes. I can't hear you. After great pain a formal feeling comes. Still can't hear you.

Looking for meaning in all the wrong places. I turned on the light and the darkness disappeared but not the glass door I had walked into. I just really like jazz. She says she doesn't understand me but I'm not convinced.

What came before now, what led to now, indeed a preparation for now. I keep walking, paying attention, keeping track of the time that keeps passing while I keep my thoughts to myself.

I'LL BE THERE

I limp and no one notices, a secret limp. Without faith in gardens, observe the flowers. Alone at home, startled by a voice saying find peace in yourself. Written months ago in my notebook, the phrase chain of events.

A realm is a realm is a realm. In the conversation, no undertone of uncertainty, I lose interest. Her lovely smile not meant for me, for the person entering behind me, and I hadn't even heard the footsteps.

I didn't come all this way just to turn around and go back. Doubt helps me to transcend. I called him heartless, he suffered a heart attack. I neither believe in nor believe that, still my brain vibrates. The wind doesn't care if I take refuge in being completely unreliable. I arrived late, looking gleefully exhausted.

For days the phrase, dawn taxi, dawn taxi. Finally I asked the taxi service to be picked up at dawn. What time would you like to be picked up and what is your destination? We need a specific time and destination. At dawn, to be driven around the city at dawn. Went nowhere. .

The sudden impulse to send well-wishes to all my friends. Haunted by nostalgia, I embrace my own ghostliness. A secret smile and no secret. You may borrow an umbrella. I have several. This one here's my favourite umbrella, you may borrow my favourite umbrella.

She doesn't exist, I know she has never existed, no limits to knowing. Silence has taken hold of me and no one wonders why. Startled by the church bells, I trip on the pavement. Hey old man, what happened, how come you're so old?

I don't belong, knowing I don't belong I now belong because I know I don't belong. Why do I need a symbol of our friendship? A planned rendezvous, she phones to say she had changed her mind. Have I heard clearly, asking changed your what, what did you change?.

Everybody gets up to leave, chairs pushed back along the wooden floor.

THAT'S THAT

At the door, glancing behind me, lights out, shutters closed, will I be returning to the very same darkness? Notes are a nuisance if I wait too long to read them. How come you're dressed all in white? Tomorrow is another day.

Down at the harbor, waiting for my ship to come in, I envision my ship out there on the ocean, a ghost ship, all the sailors crazy drunken ragged ghosts, ghosts with nothing to lose, hilariously aware of their destiny, lost at sea, lost at sea, dancing to the rhythm of the mighty waves. Ship ahoy! I exclaim.

We argued, we just argued. I like the quietness of museums. In the long run history is all about loss so let's stop now. My hands started to sweat, searching my pockets, searching for the reason. My body a temple of languor in which no one but me can ever worship. My languor will outlive me, of that I'm certain. Oh the languor of certainty!

Footsteps, I hear my footsteps, though I can remember neither where I've been nor where I'm going. Meditation, my favorite form of faking it. Anybody here? I'm here, I'm the source of being here. I'm also the source of elsewhere. Where were you when I needed you? Let's go on from where we are until I discover the source of being nowhere. Will my silhouette ever take my place.

Satisfaction guaranteed and today is not yesterday. I stay open until closing time which never arrives. You and your longing, me and my shortcomings. I don't mind waiting and I never run for the bus. Why do you keep asking when I've already told you. Enough said but I thought we had a future. Smoke in the wind, the nature of smoke.

What do I do now? Now has already passed. Then what should I do when? Some people like to look in the direction they've been, others in the direction they're going. I don't get around much so come on over. I've changed and I can change back to the way I used to be, at least for now.

A glass of wine, I say to the waitress. Please leave a menu, I might want to order something to eat. Make that two menus, a friend will soon be joining me. She gives me the look which says same as last time when no one came. Soon you will come along.

The old guy in the apartment next door, all we ever talk about is his waiting to die, waiting for Mr. Death to knock on his door. Coming home drunk late at night, I pause at his door. shall I knock? At this ungodly hour, who do I think I am?

I had known, known all along, nonetheless I said If only I had known, just to enjoy my voice saying if only. I am sending this message from the passing moment, the same passing moment that's always the same.